THE GRAND GRIMOIRE

ALSO KNOWN AS

THE RED DRAGON

Copyright © 2019

Éditions Unicursal Publishers
www.unicursalpub.com

ISBN 978-2-89806-070-0

First Edition, Samhain 2019

All Rights Reserved for All Countries.

THE GRAND GRIMOIRE

WITH THE

GREAT CLAVICLE OF SOLOMON

ALSO KNOWN AS

THE RED DRAGON,

OR THE ART OF CONTROLLING CELESTIAL, Aerial, Terrestrial, and Infernal Spirits;

WITH THE TRUE SECRET Of Speaking with the Dead, winning whenever playing the Lottery, discovering hidden Treasure, etc.

1521

PRELUDE

The man who wail under the overwhelming weight of the prejudices of presumption, will have a hard time persuading himself that it has been possible for me to enclose in such a small collection the essence of more than twenty books, which by their tell and retell and ambiguities, have made access to philosophical operations almost impracticable, but that the unbeliever and the forewarned take the trouble to follow step by step the road that I trace to them, and they will see the truth banish from their Spirit the fear that can result from having lots of fruitful trials, being made out of season, or on imperfect hints.

It is still in vain that one believes that it is not possible to make similar operations without engaging one's conscience, one need only to take a glimpse on the life of St. Cyprien to be convinced of the opposite.

I dare to flatter myself that scientists attached to the mysteries of Divine science, named Occult, will regard this Book as the most precious Treasure of the universe.

FIRST CHAPTER

This Book is so rare and sought after in our country it has been called, by our Rabbis, the true Great Work. They were the ones who left us this precious original that many charlatans uselessly wanted to counterfeit, attempting to imitate the truth that they never found, in order to swindle ingenuous individuals who have faith in initial encounters without seeking their true Source.

This manuscript has been copied from various writings of the great King Solomon. This great king spent all of his days in the most difficult search and in the most obscure and unexpected secrets. In the end he succeeded in all of his endeavors and he reached his goal of penetrating the most profound dwelling of the Spirits, whom he obliged to obey him by the power of his talisman, the clavicle, since who else but this powerful genius would have dared bring to light the thundering words that he made use of to constrain the rebel Spirits to his will, having penetrated up to the celestial beings to learn more thoroughly the secrets and the powerful words that have the force of a terrible and respected God?

This great King discovered the secrets of which the great Divinity made use, and then enabled us to understand the influence of the stars, the constellation of the planets. To prepare the fulminating (or Conjurer's) rod, with its effects which make the Spirits tremble and of which God made use of to arm the angel who expelled Adam and Eve from the Garden of Eden; with which God struck down the Rebel Angels, precipitating their pride (or imagination) into the most horrendous abyss. With the power of this rod clouds are formed, hurricanes are dispersed and one can make them fall on the part of the earth that one desires.

Hereby follows the true words spoken from him mouth, which I followed point by point, and that I had all the leisure and possible satisfaction, because I had the joy to attain success in my undertakings.

Signed: Antonio Venitiana
          del Rabina.

CHAPTER II

O weak men and mortals! Tremble at your temerity when you blindly think that you possess such a profound science.

You are taking your Spirit beyond its spheres. Learn from me that before undertaking this work it is necessary to be steadfast, constant and most careful to observe exactly, point by point, everything that I will tell you (without which) everything would rebound to your disadvantage, confusion and total loss. If, to the contrary, you comply exactly that which I tell you, you will leave behind your baseness and indigence and you will have full success in all of your enterprises.

Arm yourselves then with intrepidation, prudence and virtuosity in order to succeed at this great and immense task, at which I have spent 67 years working day and night. To succeed at this great goal it is necessary to do exactly that which I will hereby indicate.

Principio

You will pass a quarter of a month abstaining from the company of the opposite sex, so as to not fall into impurity.

Begin the quarter of a month by promising to the great ADONAY, who is the leader of all of the Spirits to have two meals a day every 24 hours of the above-mentioned quarter month, during which you will eat at midday and midnight, or at seven in the morning and seven in the evening, reciting the following prayer before dining for this entire period.

The manner in which one can make any sort of Spirit appear, reciting the great invocation that you will find in this book. So also, the true method of preparation.

Prayer

I *implore you, O great and powerful* ADONAY, *head of all Spirits. I implore you O ELOHIM I implore you O JEHOVA, O great King ADONAY, condescend to be favorable. So it shall be. Amen.*

Then eat your meals, and don't undress, and sleep as little as possible for the prescribed quarter of a month, continually thinking of your undertaking and putting all of your faith and hope in the infinite good of the Great ADONAY.

The second day of this period, you will buy a bloodstone called Ematille from the druggist and you will always carry it with you and it will preserve you from all fears and worries since the Spirit that you intend to bring into your servitude will do all that he can to dissuade you from your undertaking, believing with these means to liberate himself and thereby break the twines of the net that you begin to fasten around him. This project must be undertaken only by one other person, including the Karcist, the one who must speak to the Spirit, keeping in his hand the fulminating wand.

It is essential to choose a solitary location for this operation, which is far from any uproar, so that the operator is not interrupted. Following this, you will buy a young virgin kid, that on the third day of the quarter you will adorn with a garland of vervain (or, the sacred herb) which you will attach to his head with a green ribbon. Then you will transport it to the place that has been chosen for your operation; your right arm will be bare to the shoulder, armed with a blade of pure steel, a fire of white wood will be lit, you will say the following words with hope and resolve.

First Offering

I offer you this victim, O great ADONAY, ELOHIM, ARIEL and JEHOVA, and this in the honor, glory and power of your supe-

rior and to all if the Spirits, be so kind, O great ADONAY, as to appreciate it. Amen.

Following this you will skin the kid and take its skin, putting the rest of it in the fire until it is reduced to ashes, which you will gather and throw to the rising Sun pronouncing the following words:

It is for the honor, glory and power of your name, O ADONAY, ELOHIM, ARIEL and JEHOVA, that I shed the blood of this victim. Deign yourself to accept these ashes, O great ADONAY.

While the sacrifice burns, rejoice in the honor and glory of the great ADONAY, ELOHIM, ARIEL and JEHOVA taking care to conserve the kids skin to make the round, or the grand Cabalistic Circle in which you will stay the day of the great undertaking.

CHAPTER III

Containing the true composition of the Mysterious or Fulminating Wand as it is depicted here below.

On the eve of the great undertaking you will search for a rod or Wand of wild hazel tree that has not yet born fruit, at the highest point of the sought-after branch there should be a second little branch in the form of a fork with two ends; its length should be nineteen and a half inches.

After having found a branch of this shape, only look at it but abstain from touching it, waiting for the following day, a day destined for action, in which you will go and cut it precisely at sunrise, and denude it of its leaves and small twigs, if there are any of these and with the same blade that was used to skin the sacrifice, which will still be tainted with its blood; you will cut it when the Sun starts to break forth on this hemisphere, pronouncing the following words:

I beseech you, O great ADONAY, ELOHIM, ARIEL and JEHOVA to be favorable and to give this rod that I am cutting the strength of Jacob and the virtue of Moses and that of the great Joshua; and I beseech you, O great ADONAY, ELOHIM, ARIEL and JEHOVA to enclose in this rod all the power of Samson, the righteous rage of Emmanuel and the Thunderbolt of ZARIATNATMICK who will avenge man's affronts on the day of Judgment. Amen.

After having pronounced these great and terrible words, always keeping your eyes turned toward the rising sun, cut the branch and take it to your room, then take a piece of wood that is of the same thickness as the two ends of the rod and take it to a Smith to cap the two ends of the fork with the steel blade that was used to skin the sacrifice, ensuring that the two blades are sharp and when they are fitted to the two pieces of wood, take them home, putting the two irons on the true rod yourself, then take a Lodestone, heat it in the fire to magnetize the points of the rod pronouncing the following words:

By the power of the great ADONAY, ELOHIM, ARIEL and JEHOVA, I beseech you to unite all of the materials that I desire by the power of the great ADONAY, ELOHIM, ARIEL and JEHOVA I command you by the incorruptibility of water and fire, to separate all of the materials as they were separated the day of the creation of the world. Amen.

Following this I assure you, in the honor of the great ADONAY, being certain that you possess the greatest Treasure of the Light.

The following evening take your rod, the kid skin, the Bloodstone, the two garlands of vervain, then also, the two candleholders and two pounds of virgin wax that has been blessed; take also the lodestone and two smooth Flintstones to light the fire also half a bottle of Spirit of Water and a portion of blessed incense mixed with some Camphor and four nails that were used in the coffin of a child who has recently died.

Then take yourself to the place where you have to do the Great Work, doing exactly the following, executing point-by-point the great Cabalistic Circle in the manner indicated.

TRIANGLE

OF PACTS

CHAPTER IV

Containing the True method to make the great Cabalistic Circle.

Start by forming a Circle with the kid skin that you will nail down with the four nails, then with the Bloodstone you will make a triangle inside of the Circle, starting from the direction of the rising sun; make also with the Bloodstone the four letters that are written outside of the Circle. So also the saintly name of Jesus in this manner: † JHS † between two crosses so that the Spirits can't harm you from behind.

Following this, the Karcist, who is the operator, will let his Associates into the Triangle and he will also enter without letting himself become frightened by any noise that he could hear, putting the two candleholders with the two garlands of vervain to the right and to the left of the internal triangle. That done, light the two candles and put a new vase in front of you, that is, in front of the Karcist, filled with the ash of the Willow wood that you have burned earlier that same day.

The Karcist will light it and pouring in a part of the Spirit of Water and part of the incense and Camphor, and conserving the remaining part to maintain a continuous flame that will suffice for the entire operation.

Having done everything exactly as has been described here you will pronounce the following words.

I present you, O great ADONAY, this incense as the most pure, at the same time I present you with these ashes which come from the lightest (or finest) wood. I offer you them, O great ADONAY, ELOHIM, ARIEL and JEHOVA, with all my heart and Spirit. Condescend, O great ADONAY, to accept them. Amen.

Pay attention not to have any impure metal on your person but only some gold or silver coins folded in a piece of paper to throw at the Spirit so that he cannot harm you when he presents himself to you before the Circle and while he takes the coin you will begin the following prayer, arming yourself with courage, strength and prudence. Be careful that only the Karcist, or Operator, speaks; the others must remain silent, even if the Spirit interrogates or threatens them.

First Oration

O great living God, the only and same person, the Father, the Son, and the Holy Ghost, I adore you with the most profound respect and I submit myself to your saintly and worthy custody with full faith. I sincerely believe that you are my creator, my benefactor and my support and master; I declare to you that I have no other wish but that of belonging to you for eternity. So it shall be. Amen.

Second Oration

O great living God, who created man to be happy in this life and who created everything for our needs, and who said that everything shall be dependent on man; be favorable and do not permit that the rebel Spirits possess the treasures that were formed by your hands for earthly needs. Give me, O great God, the faculty to possess them by the powerful and terrible words of the Clavicle: ADONAY, ELOHIM, ARIEL, JEHOVA, TAGLA, MATHON. Be favorable. So shall it be.

Be careful to maintain your flame with the Spirits of the wine, incense and camphor and then make the following offering:

OFFERING

I offer you this incense as the purest that I could find, O great ADONAY, ELOHIM, ARIEL and JEHOVA deign to accept it. O great ADONAY use your power to be favorable and enable me to succeed in this great undertaking. So it shall be. Amen.

FIRST INVOCATION TO EMPEROR LUCIFER

Emperor Lucifer, prince and master of the rebel Spirits, I implore you to abandon your dwelling, in whatever part of the world you should be, to come and speak to me. I command and entreat you by the authority of the great living God, the Father, the Son and the Holy Spirit, to come noiselessly and without giving off any offensive scents, to respond in a clear and intelligible voice, point by point, to all that I shall ask you, failing which, thou shalt be most surely compelled to obedience by the power of the divine ADONAY, ELOHIM, ARIEL, JEHOVA, TAGLA, MATHON, and by the whole hierarchy of superior Spirits, who shall constrain you against your will.

Submiritillor LUCIFUGE, or you will be tormented eternally by the great strength of this Blasting Rod. In subito.

SECOND INVOCATION TO EMPEROR LUCIFER

I *command and entreat you Emperor Lucifer, by the authority of the great living God, by the power of* EMMANUEL *his Son, your only master and mine, and by virtue of his precious blood which he spilled to liberate man from his chains, I order you to abandon your dwelling in whatever part of the world you should be, swearing to you that I will not give you a moment of rest, but that you come to speak to me immediately with an intelligent voice or, if you cannot come in person, send me your messenger Astaroth in human guise noiselessly and without foul scents otherwise I will strike you and your entire kind with the blasting rod as far as the bottom of the abysses and it will be with the power of these great words of the Clavicle, by* ADONAY, ELOHIM, ARIEL, JEHOVA, TAGLA, MATHON, ALMOZIN, ARIOS, PITHONIA, MAGOTS, SYLPHAE, TABOTS, SALAMANDRAE, GNOMUS, TERRAE, CELLIS, GODIUS, AQUA. In subito.

WARNING

Prior to reading of the Third invocation, if the Spirit doesn't appear, read the Clavicle as follows, and strike all of the Spirits, putting the two ends of the fork of your rod in the fire. At this point do not be frightened by the horrible cries that you will hear because all of the Spirits will appear. Before reading the Clavicle, while the noise continues, read again the third invocation.

THIRD INVOCATION TO EMPEROR LUCIFER

I command you, Emperor Lucifer, by the great living God, his dear son and the Holy Ghost and by the power of the great ADONAY, ELOHIM, ARIEL AND JEHOVA, to appear now or send me your ASTAROTH. I command you to abandon your dwelling in whatever part of the world it should be, declaring to you that if you do not appear immediately,

I will strike you and all of your cohorts again with the Blasting Rod of the great ADONAY, ELOHIM, ARIEL and JEHOVA.

If the Spirit still has not appeared put the two ends of your rod in the fire and read the following words of Solomon's Clavicle.

GRAND INVOCATION
of the Great Kabbala

I supplicate you, O Spirit! by the power of the grand ADONAY, to appear instantly, and by ELOHIM, by ARIEL, by JEHOVA, by Agla, Tagla, Mathon, Oarios, Almouzin, Arios, Menbrot, Varios, Pithona, Magots, Silphæ, Cabost, Salamandræ, Tabots, Gnomus, Terræ, Goelis, Godens, Aqua, Gingua, Janua, Etituamus, Zariatnatmik, etc.

A.. E.. A.. J.. A.. T.. M.. O.. A.. A.. M.. V.. P.. M.. S.. C.. S.. T.. G.. T.. C.. G.. A.. G.. J.. E.. Z.. etc.

After having twice repeated these great and powerful words you can be sure that the Spirit will appear in the following manner.

Of the Apparition of the Spirit

Here I am, what will you ask of me? Why do you torment my peace? Desist from striking me again with that terrible Rod.

LUCIFUGE ROFOCALE.

Query to the Spirit

Had you appeared when I called you, I would not have struck you: consider that if you do not confer upon me that which I ask, I will eternally torment you.

SOLOMON.

Response of the Spirit

Do not bother or disturb me further. Tell me immediately what you want.

LUCIFUGE ROFOCALE.

Query to the Spirit

I command you to come and speak to me twice daily during the night, or to those who have the book which you will approve and sign. I will leave it to you to choose which times are most convenient to you, if you do not want to approve the following times hereby indicated.
That is:

On Monday at nine o'clock and at midnight.

On Tuesday at ten o'clock and at one in the morning.

On Wednesday at eleven o'clock and at two in the morning.

On Thursday at eight and ten o'clock.

On Friday at seven in the evening and at midnight.

On Saturday at nine in the evening and at eleven at night.

Moreover, I command you to give me the nearest treasure and I promise you as reward the first piece of gold or silver which I touch with my hands on the first day of every month. Here is what I ask of you.

SOLOMON.

Response of the Spirit

I cannot grant what which you ask of me, if not on this, nor on any others, unless you give yourself over to me in fifty years, to do with thy body and soul as I please.

LUCIFUGE ROFOCALE.

Query to the Spirit

I am going to strike you and all of your cohorts by the power of the great ADONAY if you do not immediately grant to me that which I ask of you.

SOLOMON.

WARNING

Put the two ends of the blasting rod in the fire again; re-reading the great invocation of the Clavicle, until the Spirit submits to your wishes.

Response and Covenant with the Spirit

Do not strike me anymore! I promise to do everything that you want.

Two hours at night-time every day of the week, that is:

On Monday at ten o'clock and at midnight.

On Tuesday at eleven o'clock and at one in the morning.

On Wednesday at midnight and at two in the morning.

On Thursday at eight and eleven o'clock.

On Friday at nine in the evening and at midnight.

On Saturday at ten o'clock in the evening and at one in the morning.

I also approve your book and I give my signature in parchment which I will attach to this book so that you can use it for your needs; I also submit myself to appear before you whenever I am called and when you open the book and are purified and have the terrible blasting rod and have prepared the great Cabalistic Circle and Pronouncing the name ROFOCALE. I promise to appear and treat you, and those who have this BOOK which will bear my signature, considerately and in a friendly manner as long as you shall call me to order as soon as have need of me.

I shall also induce myself to give you the treasure for which you have asked, provided that you keep the secret forever; that you shall be charitable towards the poor and that you give me a gold or silver coin all the first days of every month. If you neglect to do this things you shall be mine forever.

LUCIFUGE ROFOCALE.

The Signature:

Response to the Spirit

I will adhere to your demand.

SOLOMON.

LUCIFUGE ROFOCALE

CENTUM REGUM

CONJURING LUCIFER

L*ucifer, Ouia, Kameron, Aliscor, Mandusemini, Poëmi, Oriel, Madugruse, Parinoscon, Estio, Dumogon, Davorcon, Casmiel, Hugras, Fabil, Vonton, Uli, Sodierno, Petan? Venite, Lucifer, Amen.*

THE PROMISE OF THE SPIRIT

CAPO PRIMO

Io Lucifero Imperatore Potentissimo Supremo ed indipendente libero ed assoluto padrone di tutto il Regno sotteraneo, dispotico Signor in tutte le mi giuridixione, formidabile, terribile, nobilissimo, al cui Impero tuto. Regolatissimo, si nuove è governo, arbitro di tutte le fortune, di tutte le Siagure, Sapiente è Sagace, et fornito d'ogni più sublime Luminose caratere Dominatore dell' Europa, et di tutte le siagure ed Asia in particolare.

FIRST ARTICLE

I, Lucifer, am the extremely powerful Emperor, supreme and independent, free and absolute ruler of the subterranean kingdom, despotic lord over all my jurisdiction. I, the formidable, terrible, most noble, rule everything in the most regular fashion, moving and governing the fortunes and misfortunes of my subjects with absolute power, wise and sagacious, endowed with the most sublime and luminous character, am the dominator of Europe and of all misfortunes in general.

CAPO SECUNDO

Prometto è giuro al nome di Dio da viventi obedienza, prontezza e sommissione al padrone di questo libro firmato e giuratto al nome suddetto, e de miei suddetti carateri, ed in virtù di tal giuramento e sotto signassione, guiro d'adedire à tutto quello che più sarà in piacere del padrone di questo libro.

SECOND ARTICLE

I promise and swear, in the name of the God of the living, obedience, promptitude, and submission to the owner of this book; signed and sworn, in the name of the undersigned and of my aforementioned subjects, and by the virtue of the oath and signature I swear to adhere to all that will please the owner of this book.

CAPO TERTIO

Piu, prometto è giuro per parte dei miei sudite l'istesso; Onde al solo legere che si farà della mia chiamata al capo primo di questo libro, di comparir subitto,prontamente in forma di bel garzone ô giovine,in aria piacouele sensa sterpitto, rumore o altro che pozza offendere, o intimorire il padrone di questo libro, rispondendo giustamente con chiarezza, senza anfibologia alle sue interrogazioni, ed essequendo quanto mi verà commandatto, con tutta realtà, e sinceritià, sensa che de bono precedere profumi o altre invocasioni, magiche azioni, ô circoli, o ceremonie, ma pensi instentamente ofermi pronto esequitore de suoi Commandi.

THIRD ARTICLE

Additionally, as for one of my own subjects that reading my summons from the first article may cause them to appear at once in the guise of a handsome young man with a pleasing appearance without making any uproar or noise or anything else that might cause my master to be offended or frightened, to respond truthfully and clearly, without duplicity, to his interrogations and to fulfill that which is commanded of me, with complete loyalty and sincerely, without spreading scents or any other magical invocations, actions or ceremonies but rather to appear instantaneously ready to execute your commands.

CAPO QUARTO

Sensa che in tali occasioni maimai offenda le compagne, o altre cose del mondo, è compito il mio servisio di subitamente partire sensa strepito alenno.

FOURTH ARTICLE

Without in these occasions ever, ever, ever damaging the countryside or anything else that springs from the earth. I will accomplish my service and leave at once without causing any commotion.

CAPO QUINTO

Piu, prometto è giuro nella forma predetta, sua universalissima servitù di tutti i miei sudditi al padrone di questo libro sensa diferensa digre de dignità od altre regioni, ma ogni quale volta, tempo, stagione, anno, meso, settimana, giorno, ora, è quarto est instante che rara letta la mia chiamata, di compartre in forma di bel giovine, e di somministrali qualsisia de' miei rudetti in servizion al padrone di questo libro, e di non partire se prima non sarà ô sara licensiato colla semplice formola o di me, o delli altri.

FIFTH ARTICLE

Additionally, I promise and swear to the aforesaid servitude of all my subjects to the owner of this book without differentiation in rank, dignity or any other division but any time, in any weather, season, year, month, week, day, hour or quarter, that at the moment my invocation is read to provide any of my subjects to appear in the form of a handsome young man to the service of the owner of this book and not to leave unless I or my subjects given license with the simple formula, either from myself or from others.

CAPO SEXTO

Piu, prometto è giuro per me e tutti li altri al nome di Dio è delli nostri misteriori carateri, segretessa, fedeltà inviolabile, sensa ponto maimai contravenire al mio giuramento e promessa.

SIXTH ARTICLE

Moreover, I promise and swear my subjects in the name of God and of other mysterious dispositions will practice secrecy and invincible loyalty without ever failing to fulfill my oath and promises.

CAPO SEPTIMO

Piu, prometto è giuro io in particolare per tutti I miei sudetti di protegere e di diffendere il padrone di questo libro da tutte le fiagure, pericoli, ed altre naturali ed accidentali vicende, ad in caso, per qualonque suo bisogno saro chiamato, di assisterlo, è provederlo di tutto il bisogneuole, abenchè non si inotato in questo libro.

SEVENTH ARTICLE

Also I promise and swear on behalf of all my subjects to protect and defend the owner of this book from all misfortunes, dangers and other natural and accidental occurrences, and for whatever he might want when I am called to assist him with anything he might need, although it is not noted in this book.

Method of Dismissal

Ite in pace a loco vestro et pax fit inter vos, redituri ad me quum vos invocavero in Nomine Patris, et Filii et Spiritus Sancti. Amen.

I leave you in peace and I will permit you to retire to wherever you please, to return immediately with my invocation. In the name of the Father, the Son and the Holy Spirit. Amen.

Orders of the Spirit

Follow me and you will come to identify the treasure.

Then the Karcist, armed with the Blasting Rod and the Bloodstone, will leave the Circle at that point where the door of mighty ADONAY is figured, towards the place where the treasure is located, and will follow the Spirit; the others shall not move from there place in the Circle and shall remain there without any fear, despite the noise that they will hear and any vision that they see.

The Spirit will then take the Karcist to the entrance of the treasure and it might be that the Karcist will see something like a big dog with a collar that shines like the Sun that will block the entrance; this is the gnome that you will drive away from you by presenting the forked part of the Rod, then he will walk towards the treasure. You will follow him and having arrived at the treasure, you will be surprised to see the person who originally hid it, who will want to throw himself over it however he will not be able to approach it. It is necessary to be armed with a sheet of virgin parchment on which you will have written the great Conjuration of the Clavicle which you will throw over the treasure.

At the same time, take a coin as a token of gratitude, and throwing first one of yours that you have bitten and withdrawing backwards, that is, with your shoulders back, taking with you all of the coins that you can from the treasure. The rest can not disappear considering the precautions that have been taken.

Be careful not to turn back despite any noise you might hear since at the time it will seem to you that all of the mountains of the world are falling on your head.

It is necessary to arm yourself with intrepidity and not to become frightened, but to remain resolute whilst the Spirit conducts you back to the entrance of the Circle. The Karcist will begin to read the Returning of the Spirit, as follows.

ENTREATING
and Returning of the Spirit

O Prince Lucifer, I am satisfied with you at the present; I leave you in peace and I will permit you to retire to wherever you please, without making any noise or leaving bad odors; think of your promise, since if you fail for even a moment to fulfill your duties you can be certain that I will strike you eternally with the fulminating rod of the great ADONAY, ELOHIM, ARIEL and JEHOVA. Amen.

Rendering Thanks

O great God, you who have created all things for the service and utility of man, we render you humble thanks for all of your generosity which has overwhelmed tonight and for all your precious favors and for that which you have granted us, fulfilling all of our desires. At present, O great God, we have come to know the extent of the power of your great promises taken when you said "seek and you shall find", "knock and the door shall be opened", since you have recommended that we help the poor; we promise by the great ADONAY, ELOHIM, ARIEL and JEHOVA to be charitable and to spread over them the rays of the Sun of which these four powerful divinities have come to cover us. So it shall be. Amen.

VALE.

SECOND BOOK
CONTAINING THE
SANCTUM REGNUM
OF THE
CLAVICLE.
Or the true manner of making
PACTS.

With the Names and Powers and Talents of all of the great superior Spirits and also the manner of making them appear by the power of the great Invocations of the Chapter of the Pacts of the Clavicle that forces them to obey in whatever operation one wishes to execute.

Followed by the Great Magic Art, or the true Secret to speak with the dead.

Following other Magical Secrets.

THE SANCTUM REGNUM

Or the true manner of making PACTS, with any spirit without them being able to do you any harm.

The true *Sanctum Regnum* of the great Clavicle otherwise referred to as *Pacta Conventa Daemoniorum* which has already been talked about for a long while, is a necessary thing for the understanding of those who want to force the Spirits and who do not have the capacity to prepare the Blasting Rod or the Cabalistic Circle that were discussed in the preceding book.

The individuals cannot arrive at their goal of forcing any Spirit to appear if they don't do exactly that which I will hereby describe, concerning the manner of making Pacts with any Spirit, whether it is for gaining treasures or for the enjoyment of women or some earthly pleasure, or whatever favor one would desire or in order to discover the most hidden, well-kept, secrets of all of the Courts and cabinets of the world; be it to reveal the most impenetrable thoughts to make or constrain a Spirit to work at night-time at whatever task; to make it hail or storm wherever it pleases you and you see fit; to render yourself invisible; to have yourself transported to any part of the earth; to open all of the keyholes and see everything that occurs in the houses of others; so also to gain understanding of Necromancy or to gain glory, to know all of the qualities and virtues of all the Metals, Minerals, Vegetables and all of the animals, pure and impure, and to do many very surprising things.

There is no man who does not become astonished at the discovery that in making a Pact with a Spirit one can unveil nature's greatest secrets that have remained hidden from the eyes of all men and by means of the great King Solomon's Clavicle the true manner of making Pacts has been discovered and that he himself made use of it to acquire many riches and to enjoy many women and to know the most impenetrable secrets of nature which one can do any sort of good deed while avoiding any kind of evil.

Finally, at least we will begin by listing the names of the principle Spirits along with their respective Strengths and Powers; following which we will explain the *Pacta daemoniorum,* which contains the manner of making Pacts with any Spirits, with the names of the three principle Spirits.

Signs & Characters of the Spirits

Lucifer, Emperor.

Belzebuth, Prince.

Astaroth, Grand Duke.

Then come the superior Spirits who are beneath the three abovementioned. That is:

Signs & Characters of the Spirits

Lucifuge, Prime Minister.

Satanachia, Great General.

Agliarept, General.

Fleurety, Lieutenant General.

Sargatanas, Brigadier.

Nebiros, Camp Marshal.

The first six superior Spirits that I will name direct their power over all of the internal powers and have at their service 18 other Spirits that are beneath them.

That is:

1. Baël.
2. Agares.
3. Marbas.
4. Pruslas.
5. Aamon.
6. Barbatos.
7. Buer.
8. Gusoyn.
9. Botis.
10. Bathim.
11. Pursan.
12. Eligor.
13. Loray.
14. Valefar.
15. Forail.
16. Ayperos.
17. Nuberus.
18. Glasyalabolas.

After having indicated to you the above names of the 18 Spirits who are inferior to the first six already mentioned, it is necessary to understand the following.

That is:

LUCIFUGE commands the first three who are called Bael, Agares and Marbas.

SATANACHIA over Pruslas, Aamon and Barbatos.

AGLIAREPT over Buer, Gusoyn and Botis.

FLEURETY over Bathim, Pursan and Eligor.

SARGATANAS over Loray, Valefar and Faraii.

NEBIROS over Ayperos, Naberus and Glasyalabolas.

Although there are millions of Spirits that are all inferior to those above, it would be useless to describe them because they are employed by the superior ones. To work in their place all of these inferior Spirits are employed as if they were workers of slaves.

Now then, in making a Pact with one of the first principle Spirits, of which you will have need, it won't matter which Spirit serves you, nonetheless always ask for the one with which you have made the Pact, whether it is one of the three principle ones, or one of their subjects which serve you.

Now you come to know the Power, Science, Art and Talents of all of the subject Spirits, so that he who you would like to make a Pact can find in each one of the six superior Spirits the power that he will need.

The first is the great LUCIFUGE ROFOCALE, the infernal Prime Minister who possesses the power that LUCIFER gave him over all worldly riches and Treasures. He has beneath him Bael, Agares and Marbas along with thousands of other demons or Spirits who are his subordinates.

The second is the great SATANACHA, the Great General who has the power to make all young or old. Women submit to him; he commands a strong legion of Spirits and has beneath him Pruslas, Aamon and Barbatos.

AGALIAREPT, General, has the power to uncover the most well-hidden secrets of all of the courts and cabinets of the world and reveals the greatest mysteries; he commands the second legion of Spirits and has Guer, Gusoyn and Botis etc. under his command.

FLEURETY, Lieutenant General, has the power has the power to do whatever thing one could want at night-time. He makes hail fall wherever he deigns and commands a considerably body of Spirits and has Bathim, Pursan and Eligor etc. beneath him.

SARGATANAS, Brigadier, has the power to render one invisible and to transport you anywhere, to open all of the keyholes and to let you see what is going on in other houses and to teach you Necromancy. He commands other brigades of Spirits and has beneath him Loray, Valefar and Faraii, etc.

NEBIROS, Field Marshal, or Inspector General, has the power to do evil to whomever he pleases and enables one to find the Hand of Glory and teaches the qualities of Metals, Minerals, Vegetables and of all of the animals, pure and impure, possesses the Art of foretelling the future, being one of the best Necromancers of all of the Infernal Spirits. He can go anywhere and inspects all of the Infernal Militias and has beneath him Ayperos, Naberus and Glasyalabolas, etc.

WARNING

When you want to make your Pact with one of the principal Spirits that I have named, begin the day before the eve of the Pact cutting a branch of wild hazel that has never bloomed with a new blade that has never been used, in the same manner that I have described in the first book, precisely at the moment that the Sun appears on the horizon.

Then procure a Bloodstone and two candles that have been blessed and choose a place that nobody can disturb you for the operation.

You can make a Pact in a room that is far from turmoil or in some hamlet of an old, ruined castle so that the Spirit has the power to transport the Treasure where he pleases.

Having returned to the opportune place, draw a triangle with the Bloodstone and you only need to do this operation the first time the Pact is made.

Then put the two blessed candles on the sides of the triangle, as is described in the triangle of the Pacts, making the saintly name of Jesus behind, so that the Spirits can not do you any harm.

Following this, go to the center of the triangle with the Mysterious rod and the great Invocation of the Spirit, the Clavicle, the Petition, the Pact that you in mind to make with the Spirit, and the sending back of the Spirit as will hereby be explained.

If what has been explained up to this point is executed with exactitude then start to recite the following Invocation with hope and steadfast firmness.

Triangle of Pacts

GREAT INVOCATION

To Summon the Spirit with whom one wishes to the Pact excerpted from The Great Clavicle.

E*mperor LUCIFER, master of all the rebel Spirits, I ask you to be favorable in my summons of your Great Minister LUCIFUGE ROFOCALE, since I wish to make a Pact with him. I also request that you, Prince Belzebuth, protect me in my undertaking; O Come Astaroth Be propitious and ensure that the great LUCIFUGE appears to me tonight in human guise and without emitting foul odors and he grant me as per the Pact that I will present to him, all of the riches which I require. O great LUCIFUGE, I request that you abandon your dwelling, in whatever part of the world it should be, to come and speak with me. Otherwise, I will force you by the power of the great living God and his dear Son and the Holy Spirit: obey now, or I will eternally torment you by the authority of the powerful words of Solomon's great Clavicle of which he made use to oblige the rebel Spirits to* *receive his Pact; therefore, appear as quickly as possible or I will continually torment you by the authority of the powerful words of the Clavicle: Aglon, Tetragram, vaycheon stimulamaton ezphares Tetragrammaton, olyaram irion esytion existion eryona onera orasim mozm messias soter Emanuel Sabaoth ADONAY, te adore et te invoco. Amen.*

You can be certain that before having finished reading the abovementioned powerful words the Spirit will appear and will tell you the following.

Apparition of the Spirit

Here I am. What would you ask of me? Why do you torment my rest? Answer me!

LUCIFUGE ROFOCALE.

Request to the Spirit

I may ask you to make a Pact with me so that you make me rich as soon as possible, otherwise I will torment you by the powerful words of the Clavicle.

KARCIST.

Response of the Spirit

I can not grant your request except on the condition that you give yourself to me for the next 20 years so that I can use your body and soul as I see fit.

LUCIFUGE ROFOCALE.

Then you will throw him your Pact, which must be in your handwriting on a sheet of Virgin Parchment, which will consist of these few words, with your signature written in your blood.

Here is the PACT

I promise to repay the great Lucifuge in 20 years for all of the treasures that he will give me. On my honor I sign this in good faith.

KARCIST.

I can not grant your request.

LUCIFUGE ROFOCALE.

Then, in order to force the Spirit to obey you, re-read the great Invocation of the terrible words of the Clavicle, until the Spirit appears and tells you the following:

Second Appearance of the Spirit

Why do you torment me more and more? If you leave me in peace, I will give you the nearest treasure on the condition that you consecrate a coin to me all of the Mondays of every month and that you will call me one day every week, from ten o'clock in the evening until 2 two in the morning. Take your Pact which I have signed; and if you do not maintain your word you will be mine in 20 years.

LUCIFUGE ROFOCALE.

Response to the Spirit

I adhere to your demands, on the condition that you enable me to have the nearest treasure and that I can take it with me right away.

KARCIST.

Response of the Spirit

Follow me and take the treasure that I am going to show you.

Then follow the Spirit on the path to the treasure that will be indicated at the triangle without taking fright and throw the signed Pact over the Treasure and touching it with the Rod take as much of it as you can. Then return inside the triangle, making certain to walk backwards, where you will deposit your treasure in front of yourself, dismissing the Spirit as follows.

THE CONJURING
And Dismissal of the Spirit with whom the Pact is made

O great LUCIFUGE, I am satisfied with you at present; I will leave you to peace and permit you to retire to wherever you wish without making any noise or leaving any bad odors. Think then, about your duty regarding my Pact; since, if the one instant you shirk your obligation, you can be sure that I will torment you eternally with the great and powerful words of the great Clavicle of the great King Solomon with which he forced all of the rebel Spirits to obey him.

PRAYER
To the Omnipotent in Thanksgiving

Omnipotent God, heavenly Father, who created all things for the service and use of man, I humbly thank you, that in your great goodness and that you have permitted that I could make a Pact with a Spirit that is a rebel of your authority and subdue it to obey me in fulfilling all of my needs. I thank you, O omnipotent God, for the good that you have done me tonight to have shown myself to be worthy to have granted to me, miserable creature, your precious favors and to present, great God, now that I have come to know the force and power of your great promises, when you said: "seek and you shall find", "knock and the door shall be opened" as you have recommended to raise the poor, condescend O great God to inspire me to true sentiment of charity so that I can spread with this Great Work a great portion of the possessions your great divinity permitted that I could receive. Let it be, O great God, that I can enjoy these great riches that I possess, with tranquillity and do not permit any rebel Spirit to harm my enjoyment of these precious treasures *over which you permit me to own. Inspire in me, O great God, the necessary sentiment to unbind me from the grips of the devil and all maleffcient Spirits. I trust, O great God, in the Father, the Son, and the Holy Spirit and in your saintly protrection. Amen.*

ORATION
To Protect Oneself from Evil Spirits

O omnipotent Father, O Mother, the most tender of all mothers, O admirable example of the sentiments, O Son, O flower of all sons, soul, Spirit, harmony and number of all orders, preserve us, protect us, guide us and be propitious. Amen.

CITATIO PRAEDICTORUM SPIRITUUM

§ 1. Ubi quem volueris Spiritum, cujus nomen et officium supra cognosces: imprimis autem ab omni pollutione minimùm tres vel quatuor dies mundus esto in primà citatione, sic et Spiritus posteà obsequentiores erunt: fac et circulum, et voca Spiritum cum multâ intentione, primùm verò annulum in manu continetur: indè hanc recitato benedictionem, tuo nomine et socii, si præsto fueris, et affectum tui instituti sortieris, nec detrimentum à Spiritibus sancies: imò tuæ animæ perditionem.

§ 2. In nomine Domini nostri Jesu Christi, Patris et Filii et Spiritûs Sti, sancta trinitas et inseparabilis unitas te invoco, ut sis mihi salus et defensio, et protectio corporis et animæ meæ, et omnium rerum mearum. Per virtutem sanctæ cruces et per virtutem passionis tuæ deprecor te, Domine Jesu-Christe, per merita beatissimæ Mariæ Virginis et matris tuæ atque omnium sanctorum tuorum, ut mihi concedas gratiam et potestatem divinam super omnes malignos Spiritus, ut quocumque nominibus invocavero, statim ex omne parte conveniant, et voluntatem meam perfectè adimpleant quod mihi nihil nocentes neque timorem inferentes sed potiùs obedientes, et ministrantes, tuâ districtè virtute præcipientes, mandata mea perficient. Amen; Sanctus, sanctus Dominus Deus sabaoth, qui venturus est judicare vivos et mortuos: tu es A et a primus et novissimus, rex regnum et dominus dominantium, Joth, Aglanabrath El Abiel anathi Enatiel Amazin sedames hayes tolima Elias ischiros arganatos ymas heli Messias, per hæc tua S. nomina, et per omnia alia in voco te et obsecro te, Domine, Jesu Christe, per tuam nativitatem, per baptismum tuum, per passionem et crucem tuam per ascensionem tuam, per adventum Spiritûs Sancti paracleti, per amaritudinem animæ tuæ quando exivit de corpore tuo per quinque vulnera tua, per sanguinem et aquam quæ exierunt de corpore tuo, per sacramentium quod dedisti discipulis tuis pridiè quam passus fuisti per sanctam Trinitatem, per individuam unitatem, per beatam Mariam matrem tuam, per Angelos et Archang., per prophetas et patriarchas et per omnes sanctos tuos: et per omnis sacramenta quæ fiunt in honore tuo: Adoro te, et obsecro te, benedico tibi et rogo, ut accipias orationes has et conjurationes et verba oris mei, quibus uti voluero. Peto Domine Jesu Christe: da mihi virtutem et potestatem tuam super omnes Angelos tuos qui de coelo ejecti sunt ad decipiendum genus humanum, ad attrahendum eos, ad constringendum, ad ligandum eos pariter et solvendum, Et congregandum eos coram me, et ad præcipiendum eis ut omnia, quæ possunt, faciant ert verba mea vocemque meam nullo modo contemnant: sed mihi et dictis meis obediant, et me timeant; per humanitatem et misericordiam et gratiam tuam deprecor et peto Adonay amay horta videgoram mitey hel surana y syon y svesy, et per omnia nomina tua sancta, per omnes sanctos et sanctos tuos, per Angelos et Archangelos, Potestates, Dominationes et Virtutes, et per illud nomen per quod Salomo constringebat dæmones, et conclusit ipso Elh rocobem her agle goth joth othie venochnabrat, et per omnia sacra nomina quæ scripta sunt in hoc libro, et per virtutem eorumdem, quatenùs me potentem facias, congregare, constingere omnes tuos Spiritus de cetoelig;lo depulsos ut mihi veraciter de omnibus meis interrogatis, de quibus quæram, responsionem veracem tribuant, et omnibus meis mandatis illis satisfaciant, sine læsione corporis et animæ meæ et omnium ad me pertinentium, per Dominum nostrum Jesum Christum filium tuum, qui tecum vivit et regnat in unitate Spiritûs Sancti Deus, per omnia sæcula.

§ 3. O Pater omnipotens! ô Fili sapiens! ô Spiritus Sancte! corda hominum illustrans, ô vos tres in personis, una vero deitas in substantia qui Adamæ et Evæ in peccatis eorum pepercisti, et propter eorum peccata morte subjecti, tuum filium turpissima, in lignoque sanctæ crucis sustinuisti; ô misericordissime, quando tuam confugio misericordiam, et supplico modis omnibus quibus possum, per hæc nomina sancta tua filii, scicilet A et v et per omnia alia sua nomina, quatenus concedas mihi virtutem et potestatem tuam, ut valeam tuos Spiritus qui de cetoelig;lo ejecti sunt ante me citare, et ut ipsi mecum loquentur, et mandata mea perficiant statim et sine mora cum eorum voluntate, sine omni læsione corporis, animæ et bonorum meorum, etc. Continua ut in libro. Annuli Salomonis continetur.

§ 4. O summa et æterna virtus Altissimi, quæ, te disponente, his judicio vocatis* vaycheon stimulamaton esphares tetagramaton ilioram rion esytio existioneriona onera brasym moyn messias sodxer, Emmanuel, Sabaoth, Adonay te adoro, te invoco, totius mentis, viribus meis imploro, quatenus per te præsentes orationes et consecrationes et conjurationes consecrantur; videlicet, et ubicumque maligni Spiritus in virtute tuorum nominum sunt vocati, et omni parte conveniant, et voluntatem meam exorcismis diligenter adimpleant, fiat, fiat, fiat; Amen.

THE MAGICAL SECRET,

Or the GREAT ART of Speaking with the Dead.

For this operation it is necessary to attend midnight Mass at Christmas and at midnight precisely to have a conversation with the inhabitants of the other world and at the moment that the Priest lifts the Host, bow down and with a frank and severe voice say: *Esurgent mortuit et ac me veniut.*

As soon as you have pronounced these six words it is necessary to go to the cemetery and at the first tomb that meets your eye offer this prayer: *Infernal powers, you who bring the turbid in the universe, abandon your obscure dwelling and retire to the other side of the River Styx.*

Then remain there for a moment of silence: *If you have your power, he or she that interests me, I supplicate you in the name of the King of Kings to make him appear before me at the hour and moment that I will indicate to you.*

After this ceremony, which is indispensable to carry out, take a fistful of earth and spread it as one sows grain in a field, saying in a low voice: *He who is in dust awake from his tomb and leave his ashes and answer the questions that I pose him in the name of the Father of all men.*

Then bend a knee to the ground, turning your eyes to the East and when you see that the doors of the Sun are going to open, arm yourself with the two bones of the dead man that you will put in a cross of Saint Andrew. Then throw them at the first temple or church that offers itself to your eyes.

Having well-executed the aforesaid, set out in a western direction and when you have taken 4,019 steps, lay yourself down to sleep on the ground in an elongated position, holding the palms of your hand against your thighs, and your eyes to the sky towards the Moon and in this position, call he or she whom you wish to see, when you see the specter appear, solicit their presence with the following words: *Ego sum te peto, et videre queo.*

After these words, your eyes will be satisfied to see the object that dearest to you and give you the most pleasurable delight.

When you have obtained from the shadow which you have Invoked, that which you believe to be to your satisfaction, send it away in this manner: *Return to the Kingdom of the Elect, I am content with you and your presence.*

Then picking yourself up, return to the same tomb where you made the first prayer above which you need to make a cross with the end of your blade which you will be holding in your left hand.

The Reader should not neglect any of the prescribed ceremonies otherwise he could incur some risk.

See the following Figures.

prononce ta demande

SECRETS OF THE MAGIC ART

To make the Divining rod and make it work

At the moment the Sun appears on the horizon, take your left hand a virgin branch from the wild hazel tree, and cut it in three strokes while saying: *I collect you in the name of ELOHIM, MITRATHON, ADONAY and SEMIPHORAS, so that you have the virtue of the rod of Moses and Jacob, to discover all that I will want to know.*

To make it work, hold it tightly in your hands by the two ends which make the fork, and say: *I command you in the name of ELOHIM, MITRATHON, ADONAY and SEMIPHORAS to reveal to me... etc.*

To win any time one plays the Lottery

Lying down, recite three times the following Oration, after what to you will put it under your pillow, written on virgin parchment, on which you will have a mass of the Holy Spirit said, and during sleep the Genius of your Planet will come and tell you the hour that you must get your ticket.

ORAISON

Domine Jesu Christi qui dixisti ego sum via, veritas et vita, ecce enim veritatem dilexisti, incerta et occulta sapientiæ tuæ manifestasti mihi, adhuc quæ reveles in hac nocte sicut ita revelatum fuit parvulis solis, incognita et ventura unaque alia me doceas, ut possim omnia cognoscere, si et si sit; ita monstra mihi montem ornatum omni nivo bono, pulchrum et gratum pomarium, aut quandam rem gratam, sin autem ministra mihi ignem ardentem, vel aquarum currentem vel aliam quamcumque rem quæ Domino pla-

ceant, et vel Angeli Ariel, Rubiel et Barachiel sitis mihi multúm amatores et factores ad opus istud obtinendum quod cupio scire, videre cognoscere et prævidere per illum Deum qui venturus est judicare vivos et mortuos, et sæculum per ignem. Amen.

Say three *Pater* and three *Ave Maria* for the souls left in purgatory.

To Enchant Firearms

Say: *God has a share in it and the devil has the exit*, and when you fire, say the following while crossing your left leg over your right: *Non tradas Dominum nostrum Jesum Christum. Maton. Amen.*

To be Insensible to Torture

Write these lines on a small piece of paper, which you will then swallow:
In paribus, meritis fria pendent corpora ramis.
Dismas et gestas damnatur potestas.
Dismas et gestas damnatur.
Ad astra levatur.

When you will have to be tortured say:
This rope is so soothing to my limbs, like the Holy Virgin's milk to Our Lord.

To speak with the Spirits on the Eve of St. John the Baptist

From eleven at night until Midnight go stand by a fern, and say: *I ask of God that the Spirits with which I wish to speak will appear at precisely midnight*; and at three-quarters repeat nine times these five words: *Bar, Kirahar, Alli, Alla Tetragamaton.*

THE COMPOSITION OF DEATH
Or Philosopher's Stone

Take a new earthen pot, put in it a pound of red copper with half a bottle of Nitric Acid. Boil it for half an hour. Afterwards add three ounces of verdegris, and boil for one hour. Then add two and a half ounces of arsenic, and boil one hour. Add three ounces of oak bark, well pulverized, and let it boil a half hour, add a 64 fluid ounces of rose water boil twelve minutes, then add three ounces of lampblack, and let it boil until the composition is good. To see whether it is cooked enough, dip a nail in it; if it adheres, remove it. It will produce a pound and a half of good gold. If it does not adhere, it is proof that it has not cooked enough; the liquor can serve four times.

To compel one dance completely naked

On Eve of St. John the Baptist, gather at midnight, three walnut leaves, three sweet marjoram plants, three myrtle plants, and three vervain plants. Dry it all in the shade, and make it into a powder. When you want to make use of the powder, throw some like a small pinch of tobacco into the air of the room where there are the people whom you wish to enjoy.

To make oneself invisible

Take a black Cat, and a new pot, a mirror, a lighter, coal and tinder. Gather water from a fountain at the strike of midnight.

After you light your fire, and put the Cat in the pot. Hold the cover with your left hand without moving nor looking behind you, no matter what noises you may hear.

After having made it boil 24 hours, put the boiled Cat on a new dish. Take the meat and throw it over your left shoulder, saying these words: *Accipe quod tibi do, et nihil ampliùs.*

Then put the bones one by one under the teeth on the left side, while looking at yourself in the mirror; and if they are do not work, throw them away, repeating the same words each time until you find the right bone; and as soon you cannot see yourself any more in the mirror, withdraw, moving backwards, while saying: *Pater in manus tuas commendo Spiritum meum.* This is bone you must keep.

To Render Oneself Favorable to Judges

Upon seeing the Judge, say these words:

Phalay, Phalay, Phalay; preside in my favor, Let your power shine. Make me satisfied.

To make the garter of twenty miles per hour

Buy a young Wolf under one year old, and cut its throat with a new knife, in the hour of Mars, pronouncing these words: *bumalhis eados ambulavit in fortitudine cibi ilius;* then cut his skin into broad garters of an inch, and write there upon the same words that you said while slaughtering it. Write the first letter with your blood, the second with that of the Wolf, and continue in the same way until the end of the sentence.

After it is written and dries, it is necessary to cover it by wrapping the garter in white cloth, and to attach two purple ribbons to the two ends, so to tie the garters to the knee braces; Make sure that no woman or girl sees the garters; also remove the garters before crossing a river, Less it loses it's power.

Formula for a plaster to travel ten miles per hour

Take two ounces of human fat,
One ounce of oil of stag,
One ounce of oil of bay-tree,
One ounce of fat of stag,
One ounce of natural mummy,
A half-cup of Spirit of wine,
And seven vervain leaves.

Boil the whole in a new pot, until half reduction, then form a plaster of it on a fresh wolf skin. When you wear it on the spleen, you go like the wind.

To not fall when you are done, take three drops of blood in a glass of white wine and soak your feet in the wine.

To be Impervious to White Arms

With the head of a needle, write these words on your arm: *Ales + Dales + Toles*. Then put the needle in the middle cross, from which no blood will flow.

To Mutilate one's Enemies

You must cut a virgin hazel wand with a new knife at the hour of Mercury, saying:

I cut you to mutilate my enemies, in the name of the mystery of the Holy Trinity, Father, Son, Holy Spirit, and under the power of Nebyros, Apeyros, Nuberus, and Glasyalabolas.

It must be cut in three strokes, then take it home, make a figure of virgin wax under the hour of the Planet of the one you want to mutilate and write with the knife his baptismal name. And on the hour of Mars, put it between two candles, having the right arm naked, saying touching it with the wand:

I mutilate you for your misdeeds in the name of Holy Trinity, Nebyros, Apeyros, Nuberus and Glasyalabolas, Aroc, Baroc, Betu Bretu.

If you mutilate three times, the person dies in the year.

SOLOMON'S MIRROR

How to Make Solomon's Mirror
† In Nomine Domini, Amen †

The manner upon which the Cabbalist Scholars relied to make the Mirror of Solomon, David's son, who had the gift of wisdom and the occult science; this mirror is made in forty-eight days, starting from the New Moon until the following Full one. You will see in this mirror all of the hidden things that you desire in the name of our Lord.

First, abstain from any carnal action or thought for the entire aforementioned time and meanwhile do many pious and compassionate deeds.

Take a shiny and well cleaned plate of steel and write in the four corners these precise words in the blood of a White Dove: JEHOVA, ELOHIM, MITRATON, ADONAY. Then put the steel plate in a piece of new white cloth and when you observe the New Moon one hour after the sun has set go to the window and gazing at the sky and the Moon say with devotion:

O Rex eternae Deus, creator ineffabilis qui cuncta ad hominis sanitatem mea gratia, et occulto judicio creasti respice me (N.N.) indignissimum servum tuum, et ad intentinem meam, et mittere mihi dignare Angelum enim Anaël in speculum instud, qui mandet, et inspiret et jubeat cum sociis suis, et subditis nostris ut in nomine tuo qui fuisti, es, et eris potens, et jus, jud, judicent mihi quæcunque ab illis exposcam.

Take some ashes made from Laurel wood and add some perfume into it in three shots saying: *In hoc, per hoc, et cum hoc quod estundo ante conspectum tuum, Deus meus trinus et unus benedictus, et Excelsus qui vides super Cherubin, et Seraphim et venturus es judicare seculum per iguem.*

Recite this prayer three times, blow on the mirror and then call out this invocation:

Veni Anaël: veni et tibi complaceat esse per socios tuos mecum, in nomine Patris Potentissimi, in nomine Spiritus Sancti Amabilissimi.

Veni Anaël in nomine Terribilis Jehova. Veni Anaël in virtute immortalis Eloïm. Veni Anaël in brachio Omnipotentis Mitraton.

Veni Anaël in potentia Sacratissimi Adonay, Veni ad me, (N.N.) in speculo isto; et jubeat subditis tuis ut cum amore gaudio, et pace ostendant mihi occulta in occulta in oculis meis. Amen.

This said, raise your eyes to the sky and say:

Domine Deus omnipotens cujus nutu omnia moventur, exaudi depracationem meam, et desiderium meum tibi complaceat, respice Domine Speculum istud, et benedic illi ut Anaël unus ex subditis fuisse sistat in illo cum sociis et satisfaciat mihi famulo tuo, (nommez-vous), qui vivis et regnas Benedictus et Excelsus, in sæcula sæculorum Amen.

After the aforementioned prayer, cross yourself and the Mirror, and this you will do everyday for as long as it takes to make the Mirror. In the end, the Angel Anaël will appear in the guise of a most handsome young man will greet you and command his companions to obey you. Be aware that 48 days are not always necessary to obtain what you intend; often he appears after 14 days, that depends on the intention and devotion of the Operator.

So when the Spirit appears to you, as him everything that you wish and request that he appears to you whenever you call him to satisfy your requests. Then you will see everything you wish to see without reciting the preceding Oration; but having anointed him with scent (the scent of Anaël is Saffron) say the following:

ORAISON

Veni Anaël, Veni tibi complaceat esse per socios tuos mecum, in nomine Patris Potentissimi, in nomine Filii Sapientissimi, in nomine Spiritus Sancti amabilissimi.

Veni Anaël in virtute immortalis ELOIM.

Veni Anaël in brachio omnipotentis Mitraton.

Veni Anaël in potentia Sacratissimi ADONAY, Veni ad me, (N.N.), in speculo isto, et jubeas subditis tuis ut cum amore gaudio, et pace ostendam mihi occulta in oculis meis, Amen. Amen. Amen.

After you have recited this oration he will appear to you and satisfy all of your desires.

Method of taking Leave of the angel Anaël

Gratias tibi ago Anaël quod venisti, et petitioni meæ satisfecisti abi in pace et placeat tibi redire quando te vocavero.

Cross yourself and the Mirror.

Composition of the ink for writing Pacts

The Pacts should not be written with ordinary ink. It must be changed each time that there is occasion to write a Pact, that is to say, whenever the appellation of a Spirit is made. Place river-water in a new, water-proof earthenware pot, together with the powder described below. Take sprigs of fern gathered on the Eve of St. John and vine twigs cut in the Full Moon of March. Kindle this wood by means of virgin paper, and when the water boils the ink will be made. It must be changed each time that there is occasion to write, that is to say, whensoever the appellation of a Spirit is undertaken.

10 oz. Of Gall nuts, 3 oz. Of Roman Vitriol or Green Copperas, 3 oz. Of Rock Alum or dried Gum Arabic. Make a fine powder, and when you would compose the ink, use as described above.

The Secret of the Black Hen

The famous secret of the Black Hen, a secret without which one can not count on the success of any cabala, was lost for a long time: after much investigation we have succeeded in finding it and the tests which we have carried out, to assure ourselves that it was positively that which we sought, exactly matched our expectations. Therefore we are completely satisfied. It is to share our happiness with all those who have the courage to imitate us that we have transcribed it.

Take a Black Hen that has never been laid eggs and that has never been approached by a rooster and in taking her make certain that she does not cry out so that you will have to do this at eleven at night, when she is sleeping. Take her neck and close her throat so that she can not scream.

Then go where two streets form a cross and at midnight precisely make a circle with a Cyprus branch, go into the middle of the circle and cut the hen's body into two parts uttering the following words three times: ELOHIM, ESSAIM, search and then turn your gaze toward the East, kneel and recite the prayer:

Prayer to the Omnipotent in Thanksgiving

O mnipotent God, heavenly father, who created all things for the service and use of man, I humbly thank you, that in your great goodness and that you have permitted that I could make a Pact with a Spirit that is a rebel of your authority and subdue it to obey me in fulfilling all of my needs. I thank you, O omnipotent God, for the good that you have done me tonight to have shown myself to be worthy to have granted to me, miserable creature, your precious favors and to present, great God, now that I have come to know the force and power of your great promises, when you said: "seek and you shall find", "knock and the door shall be opened" as you have recommended to raise the poor, condescend O great God to inspire me to true sentiment of charity so that I can spread with this Great Work a great portion of the possessions your great divinity permitted that I could receive. Let it be, O great God, that I can enjoy these great riches that I possess, with tranquility and do not permit any rebel Spirit to harm my enjoyment of these precious treasures over which you permit me to own. Inspire in me, O great God, the necessary sentiment to unbind me from the grips of the devil and all maleficent Spirits. I trust, O great God, in the Father, the Son, and the Holy Spirit and in your saintly protection. Amen.

O omnipotent Father, O Mother, the most tender of all mothers, O admirable example of the sentiments, O Son, O flower of all sons, soul, Spirit, harmony and number of all orders, preserve us, protect us, guide us and be propitious. Amen.

OTHER MAGIC SECRETS

To prevent a woman from conceiving

To prevent a woman, with whom you are having relations, from having children, take a sponge the size of a nutmeg, and soak it with pure milk mixed with a little fine oil. Put it in her left hand and walk away from her and every time you do this you will be sure to gave good results.

To find out whether a Woman can have Children

Take the fat of a dear, melt it in hot water; the woman should drink it on an empty stomach and afterwards take a hot bath. If this gives her pain in her stomach, then she will have children, otherwise not.

To make Three young Ladies, or rather three Spirits come into your room after Dinner

Preparation

Eat neither meat nor fatty foods for three days; on the fourth day clean your room as soon as you have arisen from bed, fast for the entire day and ensure that no one enters the room all day and that there is nothing hung on the walls, neither clothes, nor hats, nor bird cages, nor curtains on the windows or on the bed and above all, put freshly washed white linens on the bed.

Ceremony

After dinner, go secretly to the room that you have prepared, light a good fire, put a clean white cloth on the table and three chairs around the table and three loaves of bread and three glasses of clear, fresh water at each place. Then put a recliner or chair beside your bed and get into bed.

Upon entering the room the three persons will seat themselves beside the fire and taking refreshment and thank he or she who has received them, since, if he is a man who makes the ceremony three ladies will come, and if it is a woman, three men will come. The three Spirits will choose by lots among themselves to determine who will remain seated in the chair beside your bed to converse with you until midnight.

At midnight she will leave with her companions without you having to ask her to leave, as for the other two, they will remain by the fire while the other converses with you beside your bed and you will to ask her about any art or science that you desire and she will immediately answer your questions, you can ask her the location of the nearest hidden treasure and she will reveal to you the most opportune time and place to recover it. She will also be there accompanied by her two companions to protect you from any infernal Spirit who could be in possession of the treasure. When she leaves, she will give you a ring which will make you lucky in any game when you wear it and if you place it on a young maid's finger you can make her your wife.

Note: Leave the window open so that they may enter and you can repeat this operation and make them come as many times as you wish. You should repeat the following prayer after each conjuration:

O summa et eterna virtus altissimi! que te disponente his judicio vocatis vaycheon stimulamaton esphares tetagrammaton ilioram rion esytio existineriona onera brasym moyn messias sodxer, EMMANUEL, SABAOTH, ADONAY, te adoro, te invoco, totius mentis viribus meis, imploro, quaenus per te praesentes orationes et consecrationes consequentur videlicet, et ubicumque maligni Spiritus in virtute tuorum dominum sunt vocati, et voluntatem mei exorcisatores diligenter adimpleant fiat, fiat, fiat. Amen.

To be Lucky in every Enterprise

Take a green frog, cut off its head and his four feet. Then on a Friday with a full Moon put them in an elder tree and keep them there for twenty-one days, removing them on the twenty-first day precisely at midnight.

Then expose the parts of the frog to the light of the Moon for three nights. Afterwards, dry the frog parts in a new earthenware pot that has never been used. Take the dried frog parts, and grind to a powder. Mix the powder in equal measure with earth taken from a cemetery, if possible from the grave of someone in your family.

Carry the powder mixture with you, it will help you succeed in any undertaking.

To make a Woman disclose her secrets

Take the heart of a pigeon and the head of a frog. Dry them as above, and reduce them to fine powder. Put the powder into a little purse, and add moss for fragrance.

Put the purse under the woman's ear while she is sleeping, fifteen minutes later, she will unveil all of her secrets. Make certain to remove the purse a few minutes after she has stopped speaking otherwise she could fall into delirium.

To see and do the Supernatural

Put a gold studded plate under your tongue, it should be half the size of your thumb. Under your feet put the border of a mortuary sheet or linen and hold a quince tree branch in your hand. Abstain from having sexual relations for thirty-five days, for thirty-five is the number that puts you under the protection of favorable constellations and sorcery and with this secret one can do prodigious deeds, as did *Mousu* with this secret did supernatural things.

To make everything in an apartment appear Black

Soak the wick of the lamp used to light the apartment in well beaten sea foam, adding to the lamp oil some sulfur and Litharge in equal parts, and all those who enter the room will appear drunk and delirious.

Glue to attach Crystals

Take some wine Spirits and whitest and clearest Gum Arabic. Liquefy the Gum Arabic with the Spirits. Heat up the two broken pieces in the fire, then with a little brush, apply the glue to the two pieces. Attach the two pieces, and hold together until they have cooled.

Glue to Repair Porcelain Vases

Take two fresh egg whites, mix them together, add a little quicklime. Put a little of this mixture on the broken pieces, hold them together for two or three minutes. Then boil them with milk and the cracks will become invisible.

The Secrets of Love of reciprocal love between a Man and a Woman

There is nothing more natural to man than loving and being loved. Without invoking Venus or Cupid, who are the dominant divinities regarding this noble passion of man, every day produces material substances that are favorable to success in love.

One often finds on the forehead of a newborn foal, a little piece of flesh that has marvelous virtue in love. Dry it in a new pot, and wear it, especially on Fridays, since this is the day dedicated to Venus, Goddess of Love.

Another Love Secret

Take a gold ring that is studded with a small diamond that has not been worn by anyone. Wrap it in a piece of green fabric and for nine days and nine nights wear it against your skin over your heart. On the ninth day, before the Sun rises, engrave the following word inside the ring: *Scheva,* with a new scribe or engraver.

Find a way to have three hairs of the person who you want to love you, unite them with three of your own hairs, while saying: "Body, that you could love me, that your desires could be as passionate as mine, by *Scheva's* most potent virtue." Tie the hairs in a love snare knot around the ring. Wrap the ring in a piece of silk, and wear it against your skin over your heart for another six days.

On the seventh day, Fast. On an empty stomach, unwrap the ring and give it to the person you desire to love you.

If your ring is accepted then you can be certain to be loved by that person. If the ring is refused, rest assured that the heart of that person belongs to another and in that case, you should seek your fortune elsewhere.

Other Secrets that Achieve the Same Effect

Here is the secret that the wise Cabbalists have called *Apple of Love* which is prepared as follows:

Go pick an apple from a tree on a Friday morning before sunrise. Write your name with your blood on a piece of paper and also write the name of the person whom you wish to love you. On another sheet of paper, write the name *Scheva,* also in your own blood.

Find a means of procuring three strands of that person's hair, which you will unite with three of yours. Cut the apple in half, and remove the seeds. In the place of the seeds, place the pieces of paper. Take the apple and tie it back together, with the united hairs, using a green myrtle twig to twist together the two halves of the apple like a tourniquet.

Dry well in the oven, and wrap them in bay and myrtle leaves. Have a well trusted person put the apple under the young woman's pillow without her noticing. In a few days you will notice the appearance of her love.

Table of lucky and unlucky days

Lucky	Month	Unlucky
7. 8. 18.	January.	13. 23.
3. 9. 12. 14. 16.	February.	2. 10. 17. 22.
5. 27.	March.	13. 19. 23. 28.
1. 2. 4. 6. 9. 14.	April.	10. 20. 29. 30.
4. 19. 27. 31.	May.	10. 17. 20.
3. 5. 7. 9. 12. 23.	June.	4. 20.
2. 6. 10. 23. 30.	July.	5. 13. 27.
5. 7. 10. 14. 19.	August.	2. 13. 27. 31.
6. 10. 13. 18. 30.	September.	12. 16. 22. 24.
13. 16. 23. 31.	October.	3. 9. 27.
3. 13. 23. 30.	November.	6. 25.
10. 20. 29.	December.	15. 28. 31.

Many wise men believe this table was dictated to Abraham by an angel and that it determined his actions: he neither sowed nor transplanted except on auspicious days and for this reason everything went marvelously for him. If your ploughmen did likewise their yield would certainly increase.

Table

Prelude 5

THE GRAND GRIMOIRE
ALSO KNOWN AS
THE RED DRAGON

First Chapter. 9
Chapter II 13
    Principio 14
    Prayer. 15
    First Offering. 16
Chapter III — Containing the true composition of the Mysterious or Fulminating Wand as it is depicted here below . . . 19
Triangle of Pacts. 23
Chapter IV. — Containing the True method to make the great Cabalistic Circle 25
    First Oration 27
    Second Oration 28
    Offering 28
    First Invocation to Emperor Lucifer 29
    Second Invocation to Emperor Lucifer . . . 30

Warning 31
Third Invocation to Emperor Lucifer 31
Grand Invocation of the Great Kabbala . .32
Of the apparition of the Spirit 32
Query to the Spirit 33
Response of the Spirit 34
Query to the Spirit 34
Response of the Spirit 35
Query to the Spirit 36
Warning 36
Response and Covenant with the Spirit . . .36
Response to the Spirit 38

CENTUM REGUM

Conjuring Lucifer 41
   The promise of the Spirit 41
   Capo Primo 41
   First Article 42
   Capo Secundo 42
   Second Article 43
   Capo Tertio. 43
   Third Article 44
   Capo Quarto 45
   Fourth Article 45

Capo Quinto 45
Fifth Article 46
Capo Sexto 47
Sixth Article 47
Capo Septimo 47
Seventh Article 48
Method of dismissal 48
Orders of the Spirit 49
Entreating and returning of the Spirit . . . 51
Rendering thanks 51

SECOND BOOK
CONTAINING THE SANCTUM REGNUM OF THE CLAVICLE, or the true manner of making PACTS

The Sanctum Regnum, or the true manner of making Pacts, with any Spirit without them being able to do you any harm . . . 55
  Signs & characters of the Spirits. 58-59
  Warning 64
  Triangle of Pacts 66
  Great Invocation to summon the Spirit with whom one wishes to the Pact excerpted from the Great Clavicle 69

Apparition of the Spirit 70
Request to the Spirit 71
Response of the Spirit 71
Second appearance of the Spirit 72
Response to the Spirit 73
Response of the Spirit 73
The conjuring and dismissal of the
Spirit with whom the pact is made 74
Prayer to the omnipotent in thanksgiving . .75
Oration to protect oneself from evil Spirits. . .77
Citatio Praedictorum Spirituum 77
The Magical Secret, or the Great Art of
Speaking with the Dead. 83

SECRETS OF THE MAGIC ART

To make the Divining rod and make it work . .89
To win any time one plays the Lottery 90
Oraison to Enchant Firearms 89
To be Insensible to Torture 92
To speak with the Spirits on the Eve of St
John the Baptist 92
The Composition of Death or Philoso-
pher's Stone 93
To compel one dance completely naked 94

To make oneself invisible 94
To Render oneself Favorable to Judges 95
To make the garter of twenty miles per hour . . 96
Formula for a plaster to travel ten miles
   per hour 97
To be Impervious to White Arms 97
To Mutilate one's Enemies 98
Solomon's Mirror. — How to Make
   Solomon's Mirror 99
     Oraison 102
     Method of taking leave of the Angel
     Anaël 103
Composition of the ink for writing Pacts . . 104
The Secret of the Black Hen 105
    Prayer to the Omnipotent in thanksgiving 106

OTHER MAGIC SECRETS

To prevent a Woman from conceiving 109
To find out whether a Woman can have
   Children 109
To make Three young Ladies, or rather
   three Spirits come into your room after
   Dinner 110
    Preparation 110

Ceremony	110
To be Lucky in every Enterprise	113
To make a Woman disclose her secrets	114
To see and do the Supernatural	114
To make everything in an apartment appear Black	115
Glue to attach Crystals	115
Glue to Repair Porcelain Vases	116
The Secrets of Love of reciprocal love between a Man and a Woman	116
Another Love Secret	117
Other Secrets that Achieve the Same Effect	118
Table of lucky and unlucky days.	120

Lightning Source UK Ltd.
Milton Keynes UK
UKHW011930020120
356266UK00001B/7/P